METHAMPHETAMINE THE DRUG OF DEATH

METHAMPHETAMINE THE DRUG OF DEATH

Larry R. Erdmann

iUniverse, Inc.
New York Lincoln Shanghai

METHAMPHETAMINE THE DRUG OF DEATH

Copyright © 2006 by Larry R. Erdmann

iUniverse books may be ordered through booksellers or by contacting:

iUniverse
2021 Pine Lake Road, Suite 100
Lincoln, NE 68512
www.iuniverse.com
1-800-Authors (1-800-288-4677)

ISBN-13: 978-0-595-38440-2 (pbk)
ISBN-13: 978-0-595-82818-0 (ebk)
ISBN-10: 0-595-38440-4 (pbk)
ISBN-10: 0-595-82818-3 (ebk)

Printed in the United States of America

I would like to dedicate this book to my loving wife of 27 years, Denise. Without her support, love and faith in my abilities, I would never have been able to reach the goals in my life. Thank you Denise for giving me your love and strength and allowing me to reach for the stars.

"Wisdom is the right use of knowledge.....to know how to use knowledge is to have wisdom"

Charles Spurgeon

CONTENTS

▼

ACKNOWLEGEMENTS

My research for this book took me to many sources. Although I cannot list them all, here are some that were very helpful to my research.

First, I would like to thank Greg Falkenthal of the LA County Fire Department. Without his initial class, I may never have formed my interest in this topic. His informative class started me on my way. Secondly, I would like to thank the California Department of Justice. They were extremely helpful and open with their material and information. Much of the video and handout material was provided either free or at little cost. Their effort in slowing down the spread of methamphetamine across the nation is commendable. A third helpful source was the Wisconsin Department of Natural Resources. Realizing the threat of this drug on the environment, the Wisconsin Department of Natural Resources was proactive by providing videos and public service announcements that I found very helpful.

One person that provided many hours of reading enjoyment goes by the pen name of Uncle Fester. Uncle Fester lives in Green Bay, WI, my home town. His books on the manufacture of Methamphetamine provided me with much insight and information for my research

Also I would like to thank a person I will call Matt. Matt was a former Meth user who allowed me an interview. Without his openness about his addiction, my research would be lacking a large amount of important information.

Lastly, I would like to acknowledge Denise, my wife of 27 years. Without her support and understanding, I would never have been able to conduct the necessary research for the book. Denise, I thank you for staying with me through the rough times and being the foundation that I could always count on.

PREFACE

My research into this menace called methamphetamine started after I attended the Fire Department Instructors Conference in April of 1999. There I attended a class given by Greg Falkenthal of the LA County Fire Department. Even though his class on methamphetamine was only two hours in length, the effects his class had on me will last a lifetime. My research has included hours of internet information gathering along with interviews with former meth users. Along with written information, many videos were used to allow me to focus on the effect that this drug has on anyone ignorant enough to enter into its grip.

As a Fire Service Instructor and a Hazardous Materials Technician, I have developed several classes on methamphetamine, covering the manufacture of the drug, dangers of the labs themselves, and effects of the drug along with a glance back into the history of meth. My purpose of writing this book is to inform as many people as possible about the dangers this drug presents. My goal is that with this information, parents may educate their children and Fire Departments may prepare their personnel for encounters with methamphetamine labs and methamphetamine users. Meth is a drug that cannot be ignored. It is here now, in our schools and in our workplace. It contaminates the lives of our youth and the byproducts are destroying the environment. My hope is that the following information may also be helpful in educating the public about this drug.

CHAPTER 1

▼

WHAT IS
METHAMPHETAMINE
?

Methamphetamine or meth is one of the greatest plagues to ever hit the streets of America. Meth is a very strong and addicting, synthetically produced form of speed which uses the over the counter cold medicine Sudafed® as a base. Using a number of chemical reactions (the recipes will not be given in this book) the Sudafed® is broken down to ephedrine or pseudoephedrine. This material is then, through another chemical reaction, turned into methamphetamine. Methamphetamine is known on the street by several other names such as speed, crank, chalk, go-fast, zip, cristy, ice, LA, crystal, quartz, and 64 glass to name a few. Being considerably cheaper than cocaine, meth is also called the "poor man's cocaine." Whatever name it goes under, methamphetamine is a deadly and addictive street drug.

DIFFERENCE BETWEEN METHAMPHETAMINE AND COCAINE

According to the *April 1998 Research Report published by NIDA* (National Institute on Drug Abuse), one of the main difference between methamphetamine and cocaine is that cocaine is plant—derived where meth is totally man—made. This is a large difference when trying to establish markets in the United States. The cooks need no middle man to get the initial drug from. All of the ingredients necessary to make the methamphetamine are readily available in any city in the United States and the profits are very high.

On the first hit of methamphetamine, the user can maintain his high from 8 to 24 hours, depending upon the dose and the users past experience with the drug. With cocaine, the high can last anywhere from 15 to 30 minutes. The methamphetamine passes through the body much slower than does cocaine. Fifty percent of the methamphetamine will be removed from the body in 12 hours, where with cocaine fifty percent of the cocaine is removed from the body in one hour. Cocaine, while not a drug of choice, is still less harmful than methamphetamine. Methamphetamine is considered a neurotoxin, which means that use of this drug will result in damage or death to the neurons that produce dopamine and serotonin in the brain. Cocaine does not possess this damaging potential.

This book is not by any means trying to condone the use of cocaine. Cocaine is a very dangerous drug that can ruin lives and families. But cocaine does not posses the ability to pull the user into its deadly grip after one use. This ability belongs to one and one drug only, methamphetamine.

METHAMPHETAMINE'S ADDICTION POWER

Never before in the history of the United States has a street drug possessed such an ability to addict the user. In an article in the *Barron News Shield* dated July 5, 2005, Barron County Detective Jason Hagen stated "approximately 10 percent of people who use alcohol become addicted to it. Approximately 98 percent of people who use methamphetamine become addicted". Many of the users show signs of addiction after one use of the drug. This is caused by the over stimulation of the dopamine producing cells of the brain. Dopamine is the "feel good" drug that the brain uses as a reward to the body. The initial dose of meth causes these cells to become stunned or even destroyed. After the users come down from the initial high, they are faced with an equally powerful dark period filled with massive depression. The brain is unable to counteract this dark period, due to a chemical imbalance in the brain caused by methamphetamine. The damage to the dopamine producing cells creates this imbalance and in many cases, the only way for the user to feel good again is to take more methamphetamine. The problem now is that the body metabolizes this drug very quickly and the elusive high received from the first hit is never again achieved. The end result is that the user is constantly "chasing this elusive dragon", and before long is using the drug just to feel somewhat normal. At this point, the drug has control over the user instead of the user having control of the drug, and addiction has occurred.

Methamphetamine can take several forms, based on the purity level. Generally, the higher the purity levels, the clearer the finished product. This is because lower grade methamphetamine still contains many of the chemicals used during the cooking process. Red phosphorus, iodine and red dye, are just some the chemicals that give the lower form of meth the brown or red tinge (Figure 1.1 and 1.2).

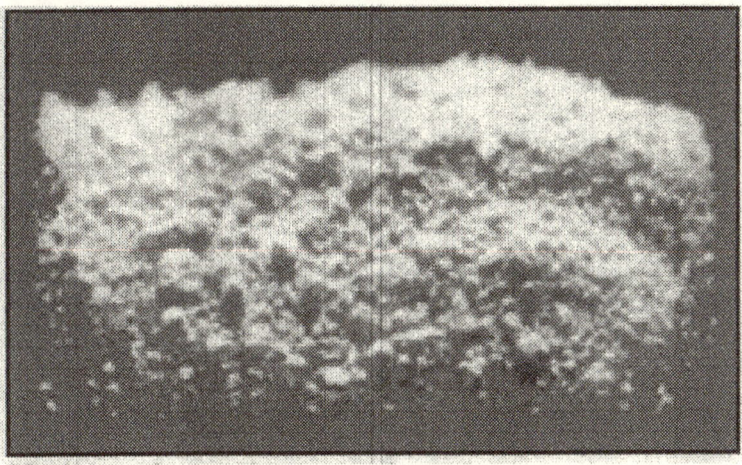

Figure 1.1 Lower purity levels

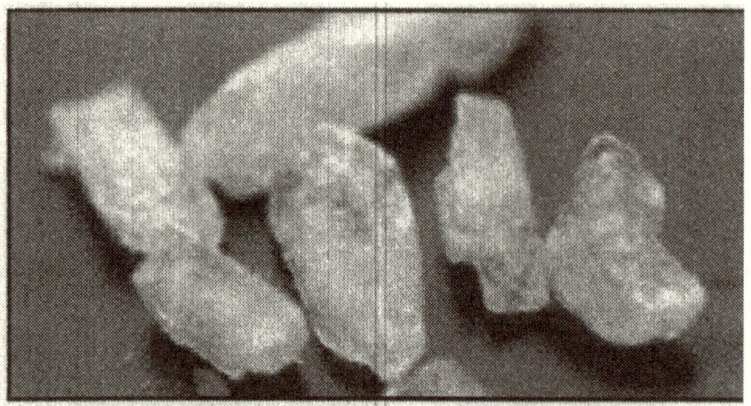

Figure 1.2 Crystal meth higher purity levels

In 1996, the Federal Government passed legislation called the Meth Act of 1996. This act greatly reduced the ability of the producers of meth to buy the necessary ingredients in the proper amounts and strengths to produce a high grade product. Before this legislation, Sudafed® could be purchased through the mail in mass quantities. Since 1996, Sudafed® as well as hydrochloric acid, sulfuric acid and other chemicals necessary to produce methamphetamine are harder to obtain. If the methamphetamine cook were to attempt to purchase these items now in large quantities, there is a good chance that he would be red tagged, a result that makes the cooks visible to the government. Other items that were restricted are laboratory level containers. Without the proper containers to contain the chemical reactions, the quality of the finished product is reduced. Due to this law then, the purity level of street meth has dropped considerably. According to the *U.S. Drug Enforcement Administration*, the average purity level of methamphetamine seized dropped from 71.9% in 1994 to 30.7% in 1999.

Methamphetamine takes the form of a white, odorless, and bitter-tasting crystalline powder readily soluble in water or alcohol. Due to its bitter taste, the ingestion method is not one of the preferred methods of use. This negative aspect of the drug has been addressed by the introduction of yaba tablets, a new form of meth that has recently hit the streets of America. Yaba tablets take the form of a small pill, about the size of a pencil eraser. To make the tablet palatable to users in the United States, the pills are flavored with grape, vanilla or lime. Yaba tablets, even though tasty, present the same dangers as the conventional form of methamphetamine. This is because these tablets are a combination of methamphetamine and caffeine. While lower in dose, the effects are the same. Yaba tablets will be covered in more detail later in this book.

Meth can be used in many ways. It can be smoked, ingested, snorted or due to its solubility may be mixed with water or alcohol producing a solution that can be injected. According to the *NIDA Research Report*, the preferred method of using methamphetamine is to smoke it, but the injection method is on the increase with the hard core users. The reason for the increase in the injection method is that users claim a longer, more intense high from this form of use. The danger of the injection method is that due to the lack of hygiene, a common trait among meth users, there is a much higher chance of disease being spread through the use of dirty syringes.

The major danger of meth is the effect that it has on the body, not only physically but also mentally. As a former user told me, "methamphetamine gave me a sense of power and invincibility." He felt the ability to do anything he wanted and no one had the ability to stop him. When he felt himself running out of energy or coming down from this high, he would just do more meth. This process is called tweaking. Many of the users tweak the drug, allowing them to stay up for days even weeks at a time. During this binge period, the user feels no need for food, drink or any other form of nourishment. The drug is so powerful that additional human needs such as companionship and hygiene are also ignored. The result is massive weight loss and no personal hygiene, which leads to many other problems for the user.

As mentioned, weight loss is a common side effect of methamphetamine use. During the binge period, the drug overrides the users need for food. This effect will continue as long as the user stays on the methamphetamine with devastating effects on the body. The body, in the absence of good nourishment, will start to drain the secondary fuel source, that being the fat stored in the body. During these binges, the user can go for weeks without food, never sleeping or allowing the body to rest or recover. This often results in massive weight loss, sometimes up to 100 pounds.

During this binge period, the user normally develops a condition called "dry mouth." This is due to the meth reducing the production of saliva in the mouth. In a healthy body, saliva is used to destroy bacteria in the mouth. During these dry periods, the user often shows a craving for high sugar and high energy drinks, such as Mountain Dew®. This combination of low hygiene, low saliva and high sugar leads to a condition called "meth mouth" where the teeth of the user rot away at an alarming rate. Many prolonged users develop massive decay and loss of their teeth (Figure 1.3). It is estimated for example, that "meth mouth" in the Minnesota Penal system is costing the tax payers of Minnesota an average of $2 million dollars annually.

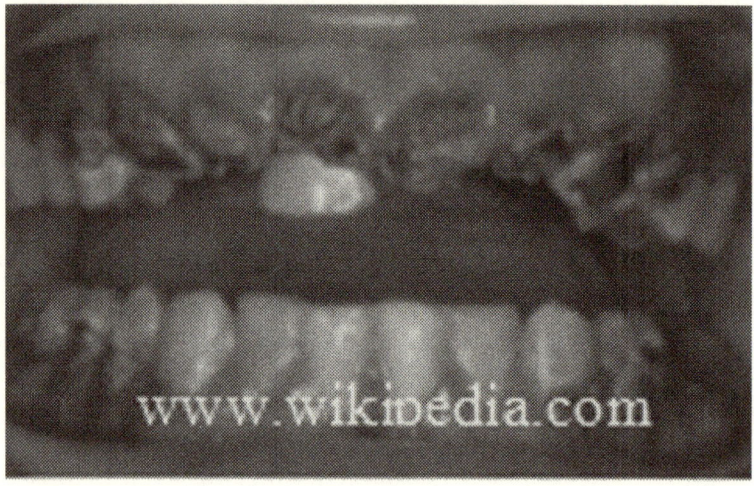

Figure 1.3 meth mouth

As if the loss of weight and teeth are not enough, long term methamphetamine users often suffer problems with their immune system. The necessary nutrients needed to feed the body's defense system are lacking. As a direct result, the body is unable to produce adequate protection to fight off disease. This lack of nourishment allows even the smallest bacterial infection to manifest into a large and ugly wound. Such wounds can often be found at injection sites and along other damaged areas of the skin caused by "crank bugs", an imaginary bug crawling on the skin brought on by the use of methamphetamine along with the lack of sleep. Some of these open, seeping wounds may become so advanced that the user may loose limbs because of the massive infection (Figure 1.4)

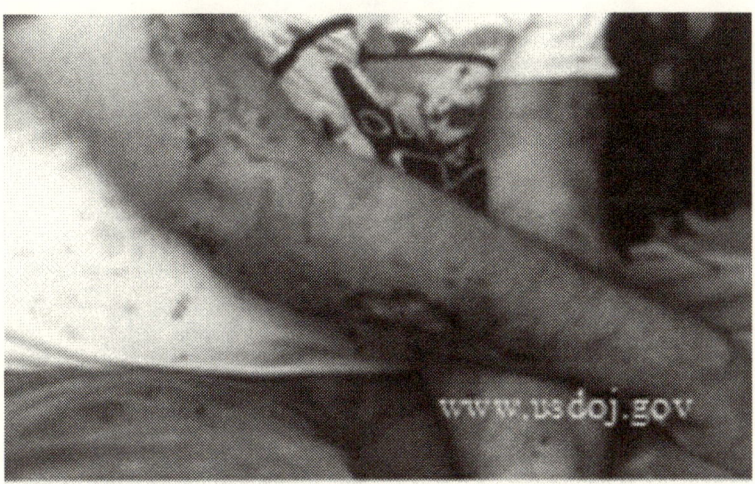

Figure 1.4 Infection at injection site

The negative effects of the use of methamphetamine are obvious, but the problem still exists. One of the main reasons for the methamphetamine market is money. Methamphetamine is not hard to make. Recipes are readily available on the internet and from other cookers. Depending on the area of the country, an ounce of Meth can be produced for as little as $140.00. According to the *Office of National Drug Control Policy*, it is estimated that the street value of meth, based on the amounts purchased and the location of the country can range from $350 to $2200 per ounce. As long as there are people using this drug, there will be a market for it. Based on its extreme addiction properties and the popularity of the drug, this market will be here for a long time.

▼

THE HISTORY OF METH

Meth is not new to the United States or even to the world. Meth in various forms has been around since 1887. This is when a lower, less powerful version of meth was created. On January 18, 1887 amphetamine was first synthesized by German chemist L. Edeleano and originally named phenylisopropylamine. After years of research, methamphetamine was first synthesized in 1919. An example of a version of meth being used in the pharmaceutical version is that in 1932 amphetamines were first marketed as 'benzedrine' in an over-the-counter inhaler to treat congestion. This use of the drug presented very promising results. It is important to realize that the pharmaceutical version is a much less powerful version than its street counterpart.

A secondary market developed when in 1937 amphetamine was first made available in tablet form by prescription for use in the treatment of narcolepsy and ADHD (attention deficit hyperactivity disorder).

In the United States, methamphetamine is classified as a DEA schedule II, which means that the drug:

Has a high potential for abuse.
Has a currently accepted medical use in treatment in the United States or a
currently accepted medical use with severe restrictions, and
Abuse of the substances may lead to severe psychological or physical depen-
dence.

There are a few accepted medical reasons for its use, such as the treatment of
narcolepsy, attention deficit disorder, and, for short-term use, obesity; but these
medical uses are limited. The key is the dosage. Methamphetamine abusers use
much higher dosages of the drug than a physician would routinely prescribe
when treating a patient.

WORLD WAR II

Abuse of meth became apparent during and after World War II when amphetamines and methamphetamine were distributed to German troops in the field.
The purpose of this action was to enhance the performance levels of the troops.
What it actually did was to produce fighting machines. These machines could
march for days on end without food or sleep. When the effect of the medication
started to wear off, more was given to keep the machine moving.

American veterans who were interviewed in the video *Tweaked by The Foundation* stated that they could not believe the ability of the German soldiers to
cover so much ground in such a short period of time. Some of the American veterans described the Germans as walking zombies, machines that just kept coming
and coming. They described the horror of shooting the German soldiers time and
time again as the Germans kept walking until the injuries caused total collapse of
the body. Speculation was that Adolph Hitler himself was addicted to meth during the later part of his command and that many of his decisions during the clos-
ing months of the war were the result of his addiction to this drug. In addition to
the Germans, there is speculation that Japanese pilots were given meth prior to
taking off on the kamikaze missions. The extreme euphoric affect this drug provided first time users gave the pilots a sensation of total power and invincibility.
This euphoric effect gave the pilot the needed drive to crash their planes into
American targets. The effects of meth were felt in Japan and Germany after
World War II, as many of the veterans showed signs of addiction to meth. To
provide for this post war addiction, 1942 saw Dextro-amphetamine and methamphetamine becoming commonly available to anyone who wanted them. At

this point, these drugs were not controlled by the Federal Government under any prescription process.

The 1960's found an increase in the use of meth in the United States. This drug was gaining popularity on the party scene and was still readily available. It was not until 1970 that meth became regulated under Federal Law. During this year, meth became a DEA schedule II drug with the passage of the "U.S. Drug Abuse Regulation and Control Act of 1970". This legislation slowed down the abuse of the drug because the availability of the drug itself was greatly reduced. This trend continued until the early 1980's when meth again started gaining popularity on the party scene. This popularity was fueled by the introduction of a very large supply source, the Mexican Drug Cartels. At this time, these Cartels started to make their move into the American drug market.

THE MEXICAN CONNECTION

The Mexican Drug Cartels were not strangers to the American drug scene. For years, they had been responsible for smuggling cocaine and other drugs across the border into the United States. The problems these drugs presented to the Cartels were many. First, the Cartels had to act as middlemen, receiving the shipments from a primary source. The drugs then had to be smuggled into the United States. This alone caused a major problem to the Cartels, as many were caught during the smuggling attempts. When meth became popular in the United States, the Cartels saw a large untapped market to move into.

The ingredients and personnel needed to make the meth were already in the United States. Once the meth was made and distributed, the Cartel members traveled back to Mexico with nothing but money. The ability to make money was very high and the chance of getting caught was low. This was a perfect recipe for these Cartels.

Prior to the influx of the Mexican Drug Cartels, many of the hard core motor-cycle gangs were the primary source of meth in the United States. During the late 1980's and into the early 1990's, as the Mexican Drug Cartels started to make their move into the American market, a brief but bloody war took place in an attempt to take the market over from the motorcycle gangs. This war proved successful, resulting in the Mexican Cartels now producing the majority of the meth in the United States.

According to an article by *Chris Eskridge and Brandon Paeper*, "The Mexican cartels control perhaps 80 percent of the American meth trade". The two most powerful cartels are the Juarez Cartel and the Tijuana Cartel. Two other players also entered the market, the Miguel Caro-Quintero cartel and the Amezcua Brothers cartel. By the late 1990's, the DEA estimates that as many as twenty Mexican Drug Cartels are involved in the United States meth market. All cartels proved to be very successful controlling the meth market in the United State

This same article also states that the power of these cartels has also spread into the Mexican government. It is estimated that a large number of Mexican Governmental Officials have been effected by the cartels. Some of these officials are:

• Chief of police in Mexico City

• Numerous military generals

• Mexican drug czar

• Head of the Mexican Federal Judicial Police

• Members of the Mexican foreign ministry

This article also goes on to say that during the transition period, many of the Mexican Officials that did not "go along" with the Cartels were mysteriously found dead. No one however could prove that the cartels had anything to do with these deaths. The power and influence of these Cartels also carried over into the United States. In 1994, Sheriffs of two border counties along with a county clerk and a county judge were jailed. In 1996 two US Customs Agents were charged with conspiracy and seven US Customs Agents, a former district director and a supervisor were brought down due to this same investigation. Lastly in 1997, three INS inspectors were convicted of taking bribes. The bottom line is that meth means big money to these Cartels and anyone who stands in their way either has to play along or face the consequences.

According to an article printed by the *Kansas City Star on 12/05/1999*, Thomas Constantine former head of the U.S. Drug Enforcement Administration made the following statements demonstrating the power of these Cartels. Mr. Constantine stated the drug Cartels in Mexico "are really more powerful than the government. The reason I say this is they make hundreds of millions of dollars, they kill hundreds of people, they are charged time and again in U.S. courts, and they are never arrested." He goes on to say, the illicit drug industry is one of the largest pieces of the Mexican economy. "Drugs bring more money into Mexico than does oil".

While up to 80% of the meth in the United States is produced by Mexican Drug Cartels, there are still small backyard labs all over the country. Many labs are "user/dealer labs" in which meth cooks make fairly small batches of the drug. The cooks use most of the product for their own purpose and sell the remaining portions to buy more ingredients to make more meth. These labs can prove to be some of the more dangerous labs. While responders do not have to worry about the Cartels, many of the cooks have little if any chemical background. This coupled with the fact that these cooks are usually high on the drug while they are making it combine to create an extremely dangerous environment for anyone to be around.

The recipe for meth is readily available, both on the internet as well as in many books. A simple internet search for the recipe or for books on the subject will yield many items to choose from. One of my more reliable sources of information on the ingredients and manufacture of meth came from a book called *Secrets of Methamphetamine Manufacture*. This book was written by a gentleman from my hometown. His pen name is Uncle Fester. Uncle Fester has written many books under this pen name. Some of his titles include *Vest—Busters*, a how to book on how to coat bullets to go through the bullet proof vest. Other titles include *Silent Death*, a book that made the news after the Tokyo subway incident. On March 20, 1995, members of the Aum Shinrikyo religious cult released toxic sarin gas in 3 Tokyo subway trains. Over 5,500 victims were injured in the attack and eleven victims died. When the cult's headquarters was raided, Uncle Fester's book, *Silent Death* was found in the headquarters and was figured as the recipe used by the cult to produce the gas.

Other books under his pen name include *Home Workshop Explosives, Practical LSD Manufacture and Advanced Techniques of Clandestine Psychedelic and Amphetamine*. Uncle Fester also produced a video called *Cookin Crank with Uncle Fester*, a how to video on manufacture of meth. On the *CBS show 48 Hours*, Uncle Fester was listed as the "Most Dangerous Man in America." The question on how this type of information can be released so readily to the public is easily answered by looking at the First Amendment of the United States Constitution which states:

> Congress shall make no law respecting an establishment of religion, or prohibiting the free exercise thereof; or abridging the **freedom of speech, or of the press**; or the right of the people peaceably to assemble, and to petition the government for a redress of grievances.

There are numerous other sources for the back yard lab chemist to use. One source is the cooks themselves. In the *Methamphetamine Fact Sheet released from the Office of Arizona State Attorney General Terry Goddard*, he estimates that the average meth 'cook' annually teaches ten other people how to make the drug. Simple mathematics will show how fast the word will get around. The scariest part of this whole meth manufacturing process is that it is estimated that only five percent of the cooks actually have any kind of chemistry background.

YABA TABLETS

The newest form of meth to hit the streets is called yaba, pronounced yar-bah. This means "crazy drug," "crazy pill", or "crazy medicine" in Thai. Yaba comes in the form of tablets small enough to fit in the end of a drinking straw. The spread of yaba has been one of the fastest-growing drug epidemics the world has ever seen. Yaba first arrived in the United States in the year 2000 but until late 2001, law enforcement in the United States was largely unaware of the presence of yaba.

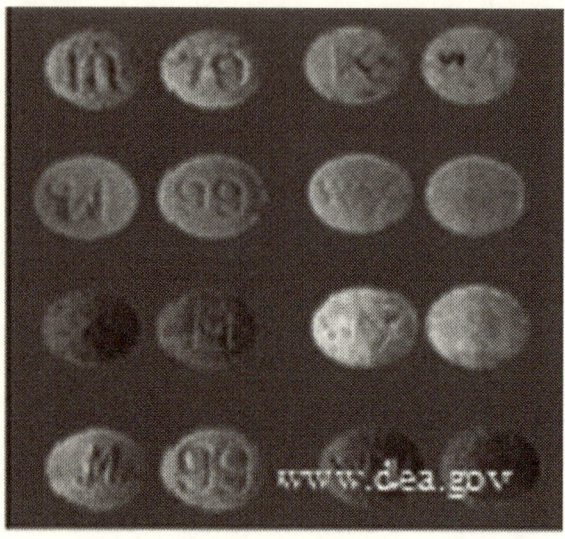

Figure 2.1 Yaba Tablets

As stated earlier, meth is normally a very bitter tasting drug. To counteract this problem, yaba tablets are flavored with either grape, vanilla or orange. The pills found in the United States are reddish orange, purple or green in color and have the letters WY imprinted into the tablets. This is an attempt to pass the tablets off as a legitimate form of medication. Yaba tablets are a mixture of meth and caffeine. They can be taken orally, crushed and snorted, smoked and even injected as they are also dissolvable in water or alcohol. Color and flavor these tablets any way you want, but the truth is that meth is meth, flavored or not.

Unlike the Mexican meth production mentioned previously, yaba tablets come from an area in Burma called the Golden Triangle. According to an article in *Cannabis News*, The Golden Triangle region, once known for heroin production, has now become a hotbed for the production of yaba tablets. Yaba tablets are produced by large drug organizations in Burma called the United Wa State Army. The United Wa State Army, estimated to consist of 20,000 members, is Burma's largest heroin trafficking organization and is the primary producer of meth tablets. Distribution in the United States is done mainly through Thai or Lao nationals or resident aliens who have immigrated into the United States. Tablets are sent from Southeast Asia most often through the mail. Some quantities are shipped by courier, air, or maritime cargo but most of the tablets seized in the U.S. arrived through the international mail system. Narcotic experts suspect that the UWSA has produced at least 800 million yaba pills in 2003 alone. This number is expected to increase in the upcoming years. The reason for this prediction is the large profit margin. The cost of production is approximately 3 cents a pill. The cost on the street is approximately $5 a pill.

One can only speculate on what effect yaba pills will have on the children and young adults in this country. Many feel that these yaba pills are safer to use, mainly due to their size and flavoring. While the flavoring and color may make these pills more palatable, and one pill contains a smaller amount of meth, addiction is still a real problem.

Another problem that may be looming on the horizon is the possibility of turf wars. The meth market in the United States has been controlled for the last 25 years primarily by the Mexicans. With this new form of meth coming from a completely different but equally deadly source, the speculation is that many people may die before the dominant force for meth is determined in the United States.

CHAPTER 3

▼

THE SPREAD OF METH

Meth started its move into the United States from Mexico in the early 1980's, hitting the counties in southern California. It did not take long for the Mexican Cartels to establish a strong foothold in this area. As stated earlier, Governmental Officials, both from Mexico and the United States were quickly brought under the power of the Cartels. Once this market was established, the spread of meth across the United States started its deadly move. From 1986 through 1994, the United States saw the epidemic spread to the north and northeastern parts of the country. States that were hit extremely hard during this time frame were Washington and Hawaii. From 1995 to 1996, meth found markets as far north as Minnesota and Iowa and as far east as Georgia.

Today, the fight against the spread of Meth has gained national exposure. Public service announcements along with billboard ads have greatly increased the public knowledge. Increased informational releases on meth lab bust have also aided in this area. While these attempts proved somewhat promising, this information alone is not enough to stop this plague. Meth is still making markets across the country at an alarming rate.

During the early 2000's, western counties of Wisconsin such as Chippewa, Dunn, Eau Claire, Pierce, Polk, St. Croix and Dane were being hit very hard with these labs. Due to this influx from the west, efforts were made on the state level to slow down the spread of these labs from Minnesota. Increase in awareness and funding to fight the problem proved somewhat successful, slowing the spread from the west. But as with many problems of this size, it did not take long for the Cartels to find another avenue for their product. Before long, markets began to enter Wisconsin through the southern route, from the markets already established in Illinois. A study conducted by the *Drug Enforcement Administration out of Milwaukee, WI* reports that there is limited availability of methamphetamine in its area, as most is produced locally by small clandestine laboratories. However, a recent seizure of 37 pounds of methamphetamine was made from out of state individuals, who were attempting to create a market in the Green Bay, WI area.

Even though the labs established by Mexican cartels are being somewhat controlled, local backyard labs are on the increase. Any community is subject to these types of labs. Earlier I stated that the information for manufacturing this drug is readily available. The large profit margin and fast turn around time is appealing to many backyard chemists. The material for manufacture is readily available from local hardware stores, so the chances of having small, local labs in your community are very high. In the Green Bay area alone, there have been at least 6 labs found over the past three years. Most of these labs were found in the post production stage, but the cleanup of the mess left from these labs is extremely expensive. According to Federal authorities, each pound of meth produced leaves behind five or six pounds of toxic waste. The average cost of a cleanup ranges from $5000 to $150,000 per lab. These numbers bring up another side to this epidemic which will be covered later in this book, that being the hazards of the lab and overall cost to both the community and the environment.

According to an article by *Arizona's Attorney General Terry Goddard*, the average cook will cook meth 48 to 72 times a year. The chance of neighbors actually realizing the presence of a lab in their neighborhood is 20%. This breaks down to only having a one in five chance of actually knowing that meth is being cooked in your neighborhood.

LOCATIONS OF LABS

Unlike cocaine labs that are very sterile and controlled, a meth lab is anything but sterile. In many cases, the cooks in the backyard labs are users of the drug themselves. Many cooks stay awake for days making this drug and due to the effects of meth, few show little in way of cleanliness. Locations of labs can vary, depending on available facilities. They can be located in abandoned buildings and hotel or motels that provide kitchen areas. Other areas of manufacture can include campers, storage units, and one site that proved very popular in Minnesota, ice shanties. One thing that all these sites have in common is all that is needed is a source of water and a source of electricity. Due to the flammable atmosphere given off by meth labs, no open flame will be present. All "cooking" is done by electrical hot plates or other electrical heating sources.

Meth labs can also be very mobile. All the ingredients needed to produce a batch of meth can be stored easily in the trunk of a car (figure 3.1). Due to the mobility factor, many labs across the United States are found outdoors in a secluded area (figure 3.2) and even in the vehicles themselves. As will be covered later, any lab that is found will be in one of three states; shipment, production or post production. Whatever stage the lab is in, it has to be considered extremely dangerous and the proper authorities must be notified.

Figure 3.1 Ingredients for lab found in trunk of car

Figure 3.2 Meth lab found outdoors

METH LABS IN OUR NEIGHBORHOOD?

How can a person tell if a meth lab is present in the neighborhood? Many times it may be difficult if the location is remote or isolated. If, on the other hand you are unfortunate enough to be near one of these labs, there are definite signs to be aware of.

First of all, the labs give off a very powerful chemical smell. Odors like strong cat urine are common, due to many labs using anhydrous ammonia as an ingredient. This is one reason that many labs tend to isolate themselves from the community. Other chemical smells not normally found in neighborhood areas are also a clue.

Secondly, a large amount of foot traffic, especially late at night may be a sign. If this is indeed a backyard meth lab, they will be selling the product, normally from the home or building. Because the cooks are normally users as well, they normally do not stray far from home to do their jobs.

In addition, seeing the occupants of the home coming outside to smoke on a regular basis is another sign. This is done as an act of self preservation. The environment inside of a meth lab is extremely flammable. Many of the chemicals used in the cooking process give off toxic and flammable vapors themselves or during the cooking process. Any kind of ignition source could lead to a violent reaction, leading to the death of the cook and anyone unfortunate enough to be close at the time (figure 3.3).

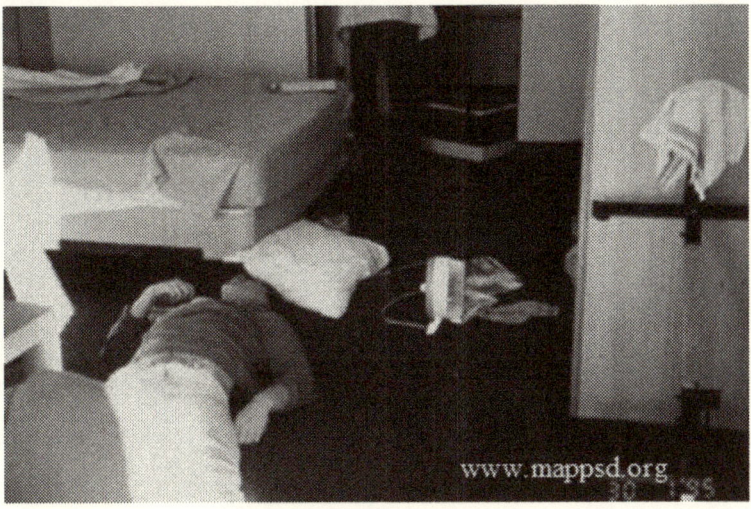

Figure 3.3 Meth lab in motel

Other indications of a meth lab may include windows that are blackened or painted with a black paint. The effects of meth use include dilation of the pupils. This coupled with the fact that meth users tend to become very paranoid, results in this need for privacy and darkness. Any light that comes into the lab is like a spotlight shining on a deer. Bright light is one thing that the meth users will avoid. Additionally, some of the chemicals used during manufacture are extremely sensitive to light. Red phosphorus for example, when exposed to prolonged heat will turn to white phosphorus. White phosphorus is very sensitive and will ignite upon contact with air. As can be seen, light and heat mixing with an active lab is not desirable.

Lastly, the area around the lab will often be littered with other clues. The area around the lab will often be littered with debris used during the manufacturing process. Items such as blister packs, used by the makers of Sudafed® or empty pill bottles are good clues. Empty cans such as starting fluid, paint thinner and Heet® among others will litter the area. Coffee filters or pieces of cloth normally stained red in color are a common byproduct of the manufacturing process. If any of these signs are present, there is a good chance that a lab may be present as well. The main thing to remember is that these labs present a very toxic and explosive environment. If a person thinks that a lab is present in their area, the proper authorities should be notified immediately. At no time should the general public try to enter these suspected labs.

CHAPTER 4

▼

THE EFFECTS OF THE DRUG

The effects of meth use were covered to a small degree earlier in this book. I will now look at the psychological and physiological effects that this drug has on the human body. In addition, I will cover the effects these labs have on the innocent victims, namely the children of the users. Since I am a father of four and a recent grandfather, I find this the most disturbing part of the research.

WHO USES METH?

Meth is a synthetically produced form of speed. Due to the effect of meth, many use this drug to enhance their ability to party or do their job. Over the road truck drivers may use this drug to stay alert for the long hall. This is why the Department of Transportation drug screens now include methamphetamine as one of the listed drugs when conducting their random checks. Meth can also be found in our schools. Many students start taking this drug to stay alert, or just to experiment. Either way, a large number of students are getting exposed to this drug early in their lives. In the article by Glen Hanson, *The Neurobiology of Addiction*, he states "The younger the age of drug initiation, the greater the likelihood the drug use will become an addiction and the more difficult it becomes to stop the use later on."

Meth is also making a mark on the party scene. In many cases, meth is present at many rave parties. The use of the drug allows the person to party for a long time, usually the whole weekend without any down time. They are able to tweak the drug, maintaining the effects for as long as they choose to. The price of this type of partying is very high. For every hour that the user is high, he is going to experience an equally as powerful down time, which in many cases leads to death or total dependency on the drug.

Lastly, there is the person who is just curious about the drug. Many of these users tend to have a long history of drug abuse. This is just another drug to add to his party list. For the most part, Meth users tend to start young. In a study found on *KCI, The Anti-Meth Site*, up to 78% of the users nationwide fall into the range of 30 years of age and under. An alarming 59% fall into the 23 years old and under classification (Figure 4.1). The fact that so many young people are users can be attributed to several reasons. Younger people tend to have a feeling of invincibility; they feel that they can handle anything for a short period of time. This type of attitude is very dangerous, especially with meth. In addition, when a person reaches middle age, he or she is normally mature enough that the negative effects of the drug can be understood and an intelligent judgment can be made. Lastly, people who get hooked on meth early do not tend to lead a long and prosperous life. Either they will turn to clinics to get off the drug or the drug ends up killing the user. Either way, the drug will take anyone who is ignorant enough to get caught in its grip.

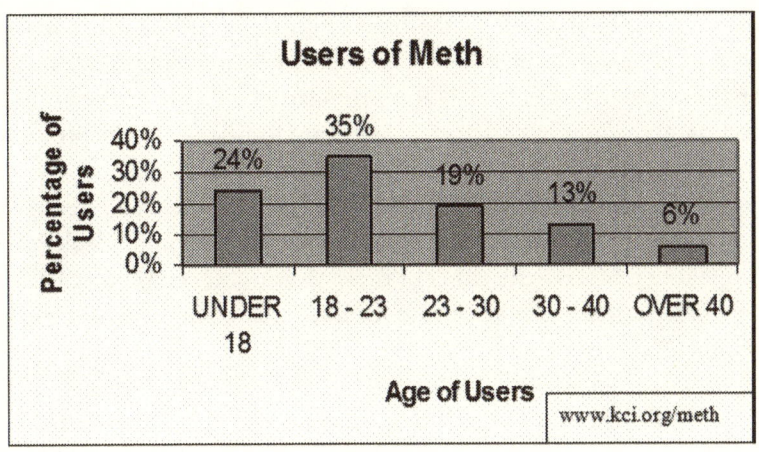

Figure 4.1 Age groups of meth users

PHYSIOLOGICAL EFFECTS OF THE DRUG

Based on the fact that meth is a high form of speed, some of the physical effects are obvious. The person will, upon the first use of meth, have feelings of increased alertness, a feeling of extreme power, a sense of well being, and exhilaration or euphoria. This euphoric feeling may last for hours, even days depending on the person and the amount of the drug used. These effects are caused by the over stimulation of the dopamine producing cells in the brain. Many of the users describe this first exposure to meth as one prolonged orgasm, an unbelievable sensation of extreme power and invincibility. One user that I interviewed stated that the first hit of meth gave him the sensation that there was nothing he could not do. The danger of this drug is that this initial high is never again obtained by the user. The body metabolizes this drug so fast that the user is constantly chasing the dragon, trying to obtain a high that they will never reach again. If the over stimulation of the system continues, this high sensation may turn to anger, fear, or agitation (fight or flight) in addition to producing feelings of panic, paranoia, hallucinations, rage, seizures and stroke.

For every high that the user gets with meth, there is an equally deep and dark down period that follows. The user may continue to tweak the drug to stay high, but sooner or later he has to come down. This down side is normally filled with depression and thoughts of suicide and even homicide. Once the person gets out of this dark period, he is unable to feel normal. This effect is caused by damage to the dopamine producing cells in the brain. According to *The Institute for Inter-governmental Research*, up to 50% of the dopamine producing cells can be damaged or destroyed by this initial over stimulation. To try to get out of this depressed state, the user has a choice. He can try to ride out the depression. This is not normally successful due to the fact that it can take years for the damage brain cells to return to normal. Another choice is seeking help at a treatment center. Here, various medications are used to replace the dopamine depletion in the body. If the user refuses to use either of these choices, the only choice left is meth. The user turns to meth as a substitute for dopamine. This indicates the start of the addiction cycle.

Meth overrides the body's need for normal nourishment. Drives such as hunger, sleep or drink are totally controlled by the Meth. Meth now becomes the control center of the brain and also becomes the reward center as well. While in the grasp of meth, the only real drive the user has is the need for more meth. Massive weight loss is common. A long term user may loose up to 100 pounds in a very short period of time. The body never shuts down during this high and the user is running at 100% all of the time. Without nourishment or rest, the body uses any reserve fuel source it has. When this is depleted, the body then turns to the fat for fuel. Many meth users will present a hollow look, sunken eyes, and hollow cheeks, as the Meth uses up the fat reserve in the body. This accompanied with massive depression and lack of hygiene gives the user a very distinctive look.

Look at before and after pictures of Meth users and this physical change is obvious. You can see the loss of hygiene, body fat, open sores on the skin (a result of a hallucination called crank bugs), along with the look of total helplessness (Figure 4.2 to figure 4.9).

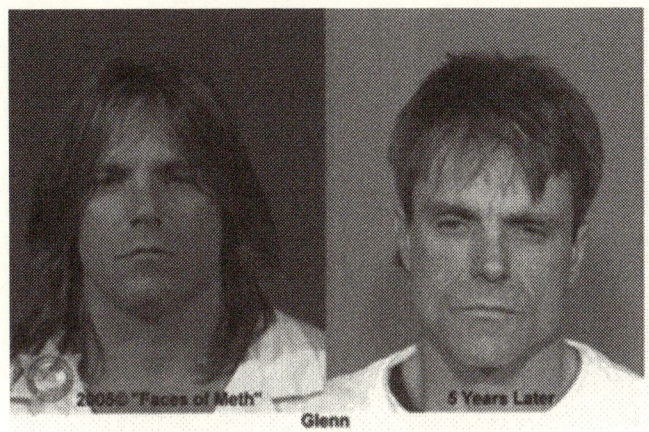

Figure 4.2 before and after

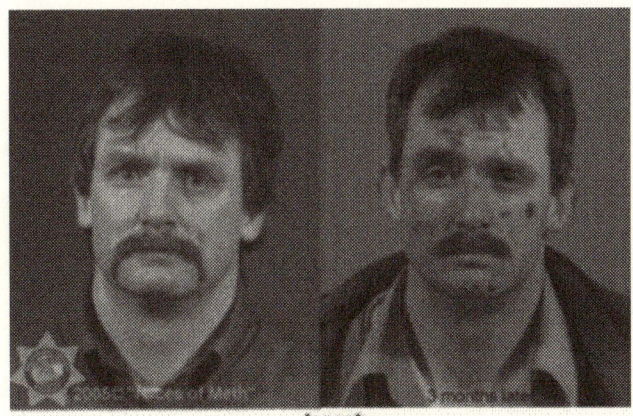

Figure 4.3 before and after

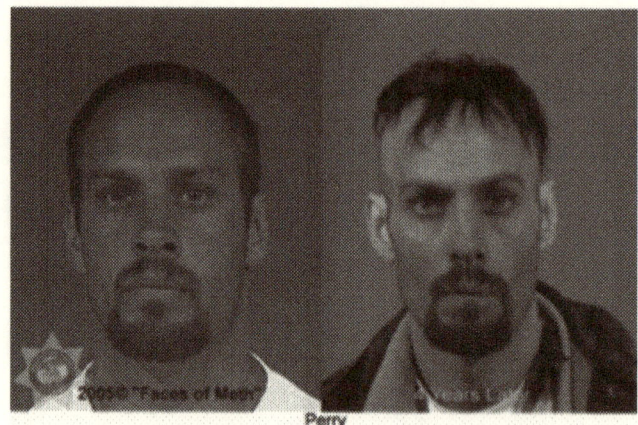

Figure 4.4 before and after

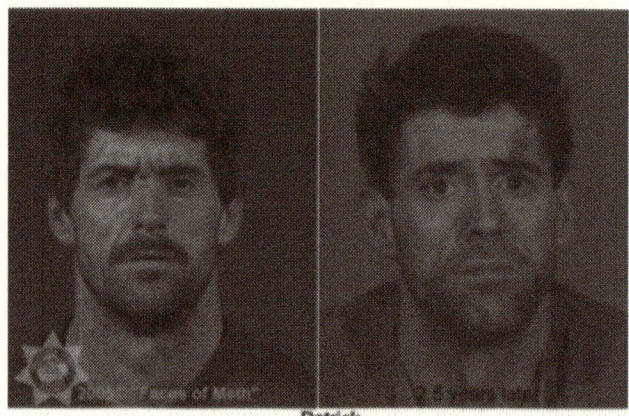

Figure 4.5 before and after

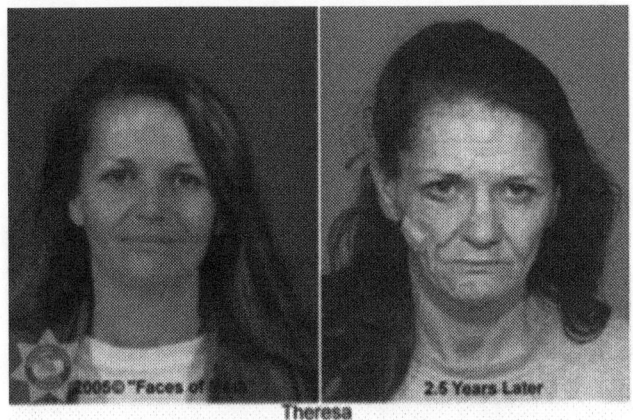

Figure 4.6 before and after

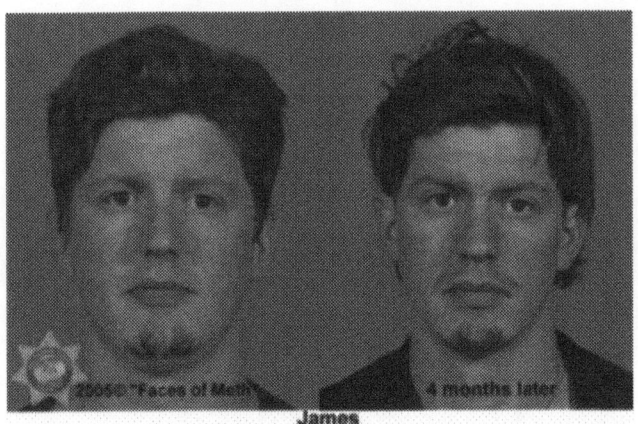

Figure 4.7 before and after

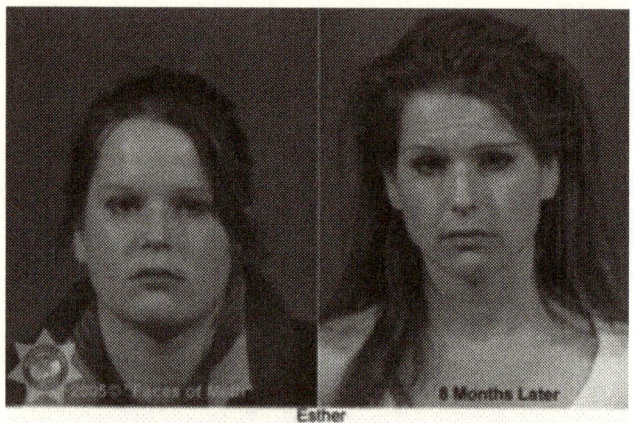

Figure 4.8 before and after

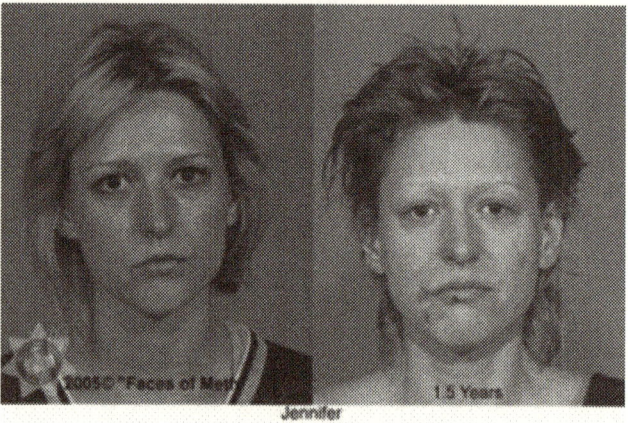

Figure 4.9 before and after

Another physical problem that meth users face is called meth mouth, an informal name for the tooth decay and poor oral health seen in many cases of meth abuse. Meth users develop xerostomia (dry mouth), a direct result of the lack of production of saliva caused by meth. Saliva is used by the body to kill bacteria in the mouth. This problem, coupled with the lack of oral hygiene and the craving for high energy, high sugar drinks and total lack of nourishment leads to rapid tooth decay. This decay is increased by the constant grinding of the teeth, a common disorder caused by anxiety brought on by meth use. Lastly, periodontitis (gum disease) is a common effect of meth use. Frequent snorting of meth reduces the blood supply to the arteries that supply the upper teeth and gums, weakening them. The end result is decay, normally below or at the gum line and ultimately the loss of the teeth altogether (Figure 4.10).

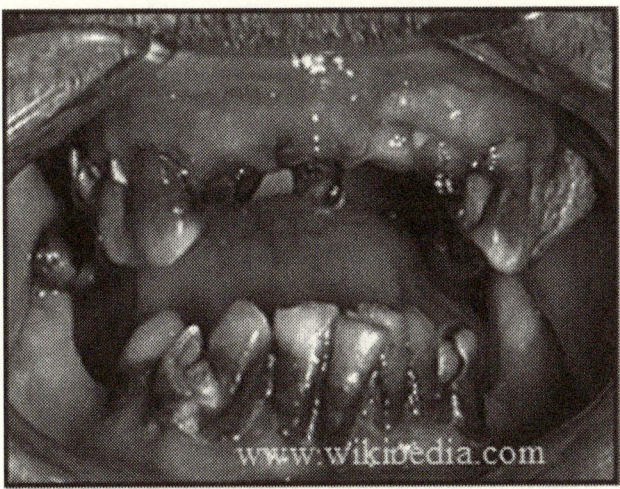

Figure 4.10 Meth mouth

Another physical effect of meth is a profound effect on the central nervous system. Because the body is being stimulated a very high rate, the central nervous system is being overloaded with the following results. First the user will experience increased alertness. He may feel that he can do anything for any length of time. The longer the user is on the meth, the more pronounced the effects on his system. Decreased appetite has been mentioned. Due to the lack of sleep and the constant bombardment of the system with stimulus, the user will develop irritability, nervousness, anxiety and paranoia. Yet another sign may be incessant talking, as the user has so much pent up energy that they use talking as a way to expel some of this energy.

The use of meth also affects the cardiovascular system. The user may develop chest pain, hypertension (elevated blood pressure), and tachycardia (elevated heart rate). All of these effects, if left untreated will ultimately lead to irreversible damage to blood vessels in the brain and may cause a stroke or heart attack.

Other physical effects on the user may include pupil dilation, respiratory disorders, dizziness, impaired speech and sores on the skin. Many of these sores are caused by crank bugs, imaginary bugs crawling on the user's skin. The user, hallucinating that he has the bugs all over his body will continually scratch at them, causing tearing of the skin. These effects become more and more evident the longer the user is on the drug. The body, lacking proper nourishment, is unable to heal the damaged portions of the skin. This results in open sores, massive infections and possible loss of damaged limbs.

EFFECTS ON CHILDREN

Psychological effects of meth include many problems that are common with sleep deprivation but that now are enhanced by the use of the drug. Problems such as schizophrenia, anger, panic, paranoia, hallucinations and homicidal or suicidal thoughts are traits that make the meth user an unstable, unpredictable person to be around. This unpredictability is evident when we look at what happens to the children unfortunate enough to be in the care of the meth user.

Children living in meth labs are exposed to immediate dangers as well as dangers that present long term, ongoing effects. Many of the children found in meth labs are subjected to fires and explosions, abuse and neglect, a hazardous lifestyle (including the presence of firearms), social problems and other risks.

There have been numerous documented cases where child abuse, abandonment and even murder have occurred as a result of children being in this environment. The major problem develops when the user is making the meth. During this time, many children are exposed to the toxic chemicals and even the finished product during the manufacturing process. The chemicals used to cook meth and the toxic compounds and byproducts resulting from its manufacture produce toxic fumes, vapors and spills. Some of these children suffer chemical burns by coming in contact with chemicals used in the process (Figure 4.11). A child living at a meth lab may inhale or swallow toxic substances or inhale the secondhand smoke of adults who are using Meth. In addition, a large number of children suffer long term respiratory problems due to being exposed to these chemicals in the labs. Many of the children taken out of the homes of meth producers show signs of meth addiction from being exposed to the environment inside the home (Figure 4.12). An article called *Meth the devil's drug*, states that of the children taken from Meth labs, as many as 85% of them tested positive for meth exposure.

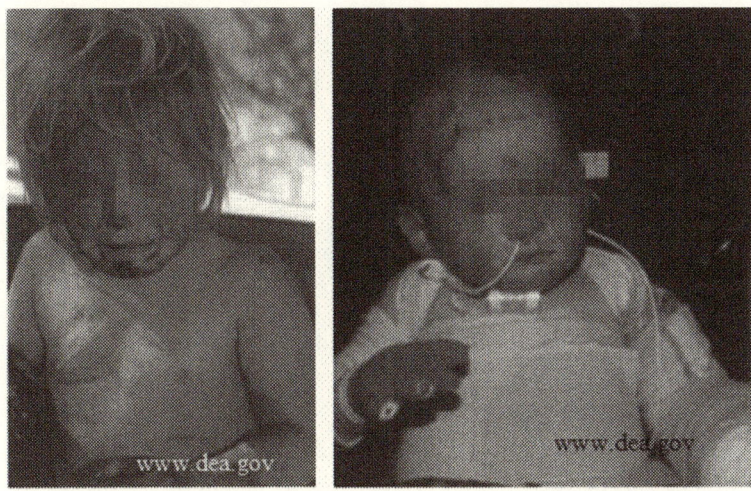

Figure 4.11 Children burned by chemicals or explosions in Meth lab

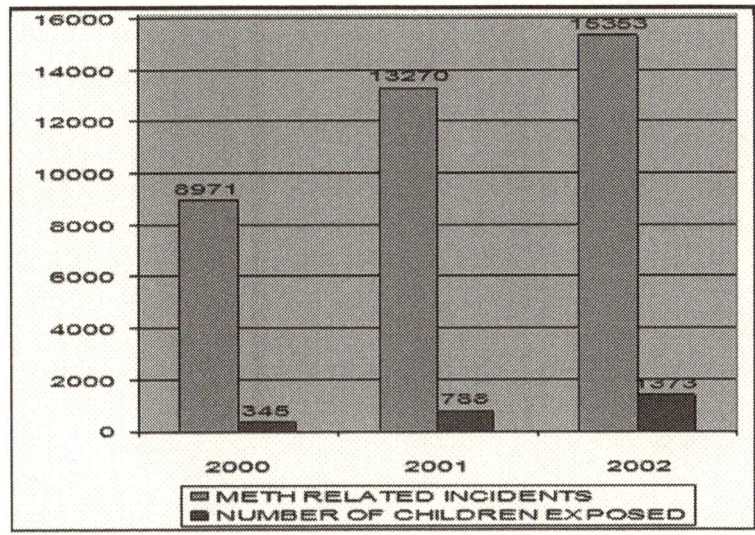

Figure 4.12 Exposed Children (information gathered by UCDAVIS Health System)

A secondary problem develops when the cookers are users themselves. The drive for meth overrides that of common sense. Children living at meth labs are at increased risk for severe neglect and are more likely to be physically and sexually abused by members of their own family and known individuals at the site.

Children are often left alone, dirty and hungry, while the user/cook continues on with their tasks. The worst problem develops when the user takes out his high level of energy on the helpless children under his care.

The major abuse of children develops when the children get in the way. The users of the drug have no patience at all. The normal response is a slap to get the child out of the way. This results in a release of energy by the meth user. This release is so rewarding that in many cases the slapping continues until it gets out of hand. The video *Tweaked by the Foundation* listed several cases where children are brutally beaten and even tortured and killed at the hands of the people they love.

In one California case, the Mother of a child was convicted of child abuse and meth use. The mother was sentenced to jail and the child was placed with relatives of the mother. Unknown to the court system, the two guardians appointed by the court were also meth users themselves. The child was beaten, burned, tied up and made to sleep in a cold bath tub. As an end result, the child was burned with hot water and then thrown on a urine soaked mattress and left to die. The two guardians were charged with manslaughter in the death of the child and the child becomes yet another victim of the madness caused by meth.

The meth lab also presents other hazards for the children. Explosives and booby traps are common at these labs. Loaded guns and other weapons are present and are usually found in easy-to-reach locations. Living and play areas may be infested with rodents and insects, including cockroaches, fleas, ticks, and lice. Toilets and bathtubs may be backed up or unusable, sometimes because the cook has dumped corrosive byproducts into the plumbing. Dangerous animals trained to protect illegal meth labs pose added physical hazards and their feces contribute to the filth in area where children play, eat and sleep.

Children developing within the chaos and neglect of a meth lab experience stress and trauma that significantly affect their overall safety and health, including their behavioral, emotional and cognitive functioning. They often exhibit low self-esteem, a sense of shame and poor social skills. Consequences may include emotional and mental health problems, delinquency, teen pregnancy, isolation and poor peer relations. Without the proper intervention, many will imitate their parents and caretakers when they themselves become adults, engaging in the same type of abusive pattern.

PSYCHOLOGICAL EFFECTS OF THE DRUG

An example of hallucinations due to meth occurred in California as well. Documented in an interview on the videotape *Tweaked*, a user went to a meth house to score some meth. Upon passing through the kitchen area, he noticed a woman scratching at her nose. The man continued into another room to score the meth and he heard a scream. Upon going back to the kitchen, he witnessed the woman with a knife in her hand and her nose on the floor. She had hallucinations called "crank bugs". This occurs when the meth user goes without sleep for some time. They then start to imagine bugs crawling all over their body. The meth user scratches at these "bugs," often for hours at a time. The result is large scratches and scrapes, where even large portions of the skin are torn from body (Figure 4.13).

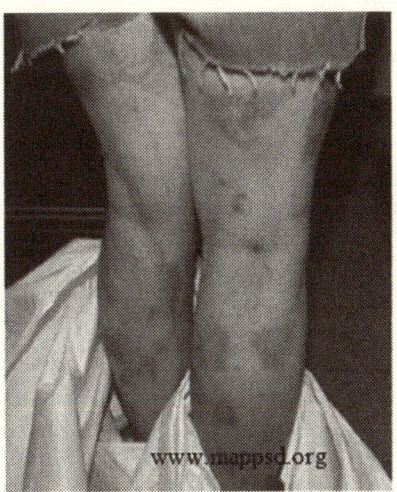

Figure 4.13 Results of Crank Bugs

EFFECTS ON THE UNBORN

Meth also has the ability to reach into the next generation. Women of childbearing age or who may be pregnant and who use meth may be affecting the unborn child. *Arizona State Attorney General Terry Goddard* states that prenatal exposure to meth causes infants to be six times more likely to be born with birth defects. Some of these effects are:

- Effects on the brain and spinal cord:
  - Spina bifida

- Effects on the heart:
  - Underdeveloped heart muscle

- Effects on the kidneys:
  - malformation of the kidneys

- Effects on the intestines:
  - Gastroschesis—a hole in the abdomen, all of the intestines are outside of the body

- Effects on the skeletal system:
  - Club foot, developmental abnormalities or missing parts of their arms or legs

- Other effects:
  - Sleeping disorders due to damage to transmitters in the brain
  - Learning disabilities
  - Hyperactivity

INTERVIEW AND OBSERVANCE OF A METH USER

Even after the meth user is clean from the drug, the effects of the abuse are long lasting. I conducted an interview with a former meth user on November 11, 2002. The person I interviewed, I will call him Matt, is a 43 year old male user. He has a long history of drug abuse, starting his abuse at the age of 25. He was one of the few that could control the use of the drug. He admitted to using meth for 10 years on a steady basis. He has now been clean for the past five years. His main motivation for seeking help was the fact that he was offered a job with the State Government. Due to random drug checks, he had no choice but to seek help.

I asked Matt how he actually got clean. He stated that he had to go to a treatment center where they used medication to replace the dopamine depletion in his system. In addition, he had to change his life style completely. He explained that when you were using meth, you did not really have friends anymore. What you had were drug acquaintances, people who shared the same dependencies as you did. To rid himself of his addiction, he had to rid himself of these acquaintances. With the help of the medication, therapy and along with his change in lifestyle, he was able to rid himself of his dependency.

Even though Matt got off of meth, the effects of the drug still were with him. During the weekend I was observing Matt, I saw the effects of his abuse. Some of my observations were:

- Very unpredictable behavior pattern
  - Isolation tendency

- Sleep pattern very abnormal
  - Never slept deep, very shallow irregular sleeping pattern

- Mood swings very obvious
  - Up one minute, down and quiet the next

Matt would be social one minute then disappear for hours at a time. He told no one where he was going or that he was even leaving. Secondly, he was never really at rest. He would sleep, but his sleep was restless. Even though he was snoring, he would wake up and join into the conversation as if he heard everything we were talking about. He never slept more than 2 hours at a time without getting up and walking around the cabin. Lastly, Matt displayed wide mood swings. He would be up, very positive and then suddenly fall into a state of depression where nothing we said or did made any difference. He even stated that he still harbored feelings of suicide at times, a direct result of the drug.

I also had an opportunity to view a person who was on meth. I was on a family vacation to Virginia Beach. It was a cool night in July, so cool that I was wearing a light coat. There was a band playing on the boardwalk so I wandered over to see what I could see. I noticed this guy, dancing by himself with nothing on but shorts. Even though the night was cool, he was sweating profusely. He walked by me and I experienced the smell that I have read about. Meth is a dirty drug, and the body tries to get rid of these toxins. The smell from this guy reminded me of a combination of glue and mayonnaise. I know this is not a very pleasant thought, but it is a definite sign of a meth user. He would light a cigarette, take a drag, put it out and run out on the dance floor once more. He had more energy than he knew what to do with. His actions continued the same through the evening. He was having a good time and when he smiled I noticed that several of his teeth were missing. The only good part of his actions was that the dance floor cleared out rather quickly.

EFFECTS ON THE ENVIRONMENT

Meth is an extremely dirty drug, both to make and to use. According to Federal authorities, each pound of meth produced leaves behind five or six pounds of toxic waste. The average cost of a cleanup ranges from $5000 to $150,000 per lab. Acetone, acids, bases, red phosphorus, iodine and various mixtures and compounds are a result of the production process. Many of the chemicals are dumped down the drain. If the lab is outside, the chemicals are either left in unmarked containers or dumped onto the ground or into creeks or streams. This action results in severe damage to the environment (Figure 4.14).

Figure 4.14 Damage to the environment

In one documented case taken from the video *Where Meth Goes, Violence and Destruction Follows by the California Department of Justice,* a California rancher owned property that had a nice pond that his family had used for swimming and fishing. A group of meth cookers set up a shop next to the pond and produced large quantities of Meth dumping the waste products around and into the pond. This resulted in the trees that were exposed directly to the chemicals dying and the pond turning into a dead, open sewer that cost over $150,000 to clean up. Even though the ranch was large and the rancher did not often travel back to this area, he was still held responsible for the clean up cost of the lab.

Another case hit fairly close to home when one of my favorite deer hunting spots was a scene of a meth lab. This area was a somewhat wooded area mixed with clearings that allowed for a very effective hunting area. There was a creek flowing through the land, emptying into a larger river a few miles to the south. During the fall months a few years ago, a truck with several "hunters" dressed in camouflage, camped out in this area. Being public land, everyone thought that these hunters were actually hunting. Little did they know the truth of the matter. Soon after the truck left the area, local and state vehicles started showing up. It turned out that the cookers made several batches of meth and dumped the chemicals into the creek and along the bank. The area was littered with chemicals and containers from the process. It took several months and a lot of money to clean up this mess.

The bottom line is that meth is the type of drug never before seen in America. Once someone is ignorant enough to try meth, it is already too late. The drug obtains a grip on the person that will have long lasting effects, effects that will last long after the person is lucky enough to get off of the drug. The big thing to remember is that the best way to prevent the effects of meth is to stay away, far, far away.

CHAPTER 5

▼

WHAT MAKES METH LABS DANGEROUS?

There are several reasons why these labs are dangerous to the public, emergency responders and the environment. The reasons are the chemicals used in the process, the chemicals produced by the process, the manufacturing process as well as the users themselves. All of these items present their own types of hazards. Again, labs can be found in transit, production and post production. The hazards present will depend greatly on what stage the process is in.

CHEMICALS USED IN THE PROCESS

To make meth, many chemicals are needed to start and control the various reactions that occur. Some of the needed chemicals are toluene, methanol, ethyl ether, anhydrous ammonia, hydrochloric acid, ephedrine or pseudophedrine, sodium hydroxide (Drano®), sulfuric acid, iodine crystals, red phosphorous, and lithium, a combustible metal. Many of these chemicals create the dangerous environment in these meth labs. Let's take a look at some of the hazards associated with the listed chemicals.

Toluene is an industrial chemical that is also a flammable liquid. When this liquid is exposed to air, it will evaporate and form a cloud of combustible vapors that are heavier than air. This results in combustible vapors that will tend to pool in low lying areas and not readily leave the building. In addition, toluene has a very low flash point, 40° F. If the toluene is present in an atmosphere above 40° and an ignition source is present, toluene will ignite. Many people are under a mistaken assumption that an open flame would be necessary to ignite this material. The truth is that it is not the size of the heat source but the heat in the source that is important. A normal static spark is capable of generating temperatures of around 1000° F, well above the needed temperature for many flammable liquids to ignite. In addition to being combustible, toluene vapors are also dangerous to the body, targeting the eyes, skin, respiratory system, central nervous system, liver, kidneys.

Methanol goes by another familiar name, formaldehyde. This chemical is a strong respiratory irritant and can injure the lungs when present in high levels. It is also reactive with other chemicals, such as hydrogen chloride and acids. When these chemicals mix the result usually will be a fire or an explosion.

Ethyl ether is another gas that is found in meth labs. Ethyl ether is a highly flammable material and has the capability to form a flammable cloud over a wide area. The meth cook, not being able to get pure ethyl ether, will extract this material from cans of starter fluid where ethyl ether is found as an ingredient. Cooks turn the can upside down, puncturing the bottom of the can and extracting the needed chemical from the can. The vapors that ethyl ether produces are also deadly. They have the ability to suppress the central nervous system, causing respiratory distress and death.

Anhydrous ammonia is a chemical now being seen in meth labs because cookers are using a new recipe, called the Nazi method of cooking. Anhydrous ammonia is basically ammonia that has the water taken out of it. The cooks can find a large supply of anhydrous ammonia at any Farmers Coop or even in the farmer's fields. Anhydrous ammonia is added to the fields in the spring as a way to enrich the soil. The tanks of anhydrous ammonia are plentiful and fairly easy to get at (Figure 5.1). The process the cooks use to obtain this chemical consists of purchasing an empty 20 pound propane tank and the necessary hose, both of which are readily available at any home improvement store. The cooks hook the hose to both of the tanks and download the liquid ammonia simply by opening the valves. The ammonia in the large tanks is under great pressure, and the downloading occurs naturally once the valves are opened.

Figure 5.1 Tanks of Anhydrous Ammonia

This process brings a new danger to the meth labs. First of all, anhydrous ammonia is a liquefied compressed gas that is very toxic. When this liquid is released into the atmosphere, it turns into a vapor cloud. Being anhydrous, this form of ammonia is searching for any liquid it can find. When anyone comes in contact with this cloud, they will experience extreme burns to any part of the body, especially eyes and lungs. In addition, anhydrous ammonia also presents a flammability hazard. Once released, under the right circumstances, anhydrous ammonia can ignite. Yet another dangerous side effect of the Nazi method of cooking is that the propane tanks are stored and used in the lab. The propane tanks and brass valves are not designed to handle the corrosive nature of anhydrous ammonia (Figure 5.2). A new method of obtaining and storing anhydrous ammonia is by using empty 2.5 gallon water extinguishers (Figure 5.3). These extinguishers are filled with anhydrous ammonia, the same way the propane tanks are filled. Tank failure and valve corrosion are common results. Any tank found near or in these labs that have valves corroded green should be left alone. Simply by touching the valves, the valve could fail causing release of the contents. When this tank releases its contents, the results are disastrous (Figure 5.4).

Figure 5.2 Corrosion on propane valve

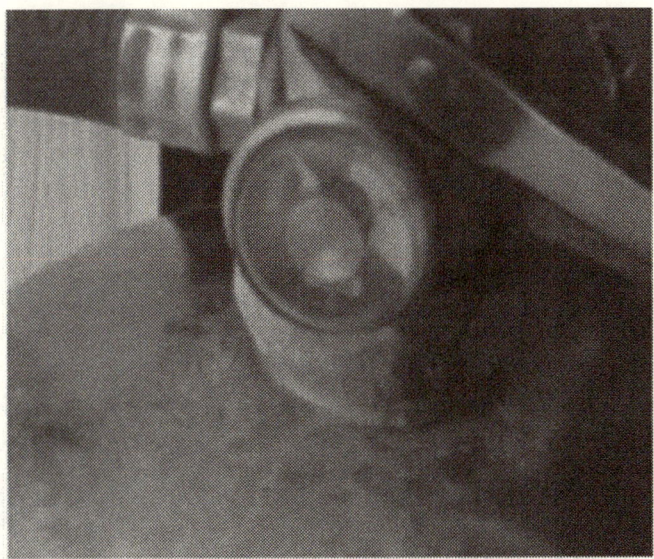

Figure 5.3 close up of corrosion

Figure 5.4 Release of anhydrous ammonia from 20 pound tank

As if these hazards were not enough, anhydrous ammonia presents still another problem. When the liquid in the tank is heated to 850 degrees F. the ammonia will disassociate, which mean it will chemically break down to two completely different chemicals, nitrogen and hydrogen. Nitrogen is a non flammable gas, but hydrogen is an extremely explosive gas. When disassociation occurs, the liquid contents of the tank expand to 45 cubic feet of vapor, filling any room with the toxic and flammable mixture.

Hydrochloric acid, also known as muriatic acid, is a strong corrosive. When used in the chemical reaction, it becomes airborne, where it becomes a strong irritant to the eyes, mucous membranes and skin. In high concentrations it can cause extreme burns to the respiratory tract, upper respiratory irritation and a choking sensation. High concentrations may also lead to laryngeal spasm and pulmonary edema, causing the lungs to fill with fluid resulting in the exposed person drowning in his own fluids.

Sodium hydroxide, also known as lye or Drano® is a very strong base. There is a common misconception that bases are not as harmful as acids. This is very far from the truth. Bases can be just as dangerous as acids, depending on the strength or concentration of the product. This material is normally found in a powder form, and contact with the eyes or skin can cause severe burns. Breathing the material can also cause damage to the respiratory track. Sodium hydroxide also has some secondary properties that make it dangerous. This material is incompatible with water, acids, and flammable liquids and certain metals, all of which are present in the lab. When contact with water occurs, sodium hydroxide may generate sufficient heat to ignite other nearby combustible materials. Other problems faced with this reactive material is the over pressurization of containment vessels resulting in failure of the container and release of the product from its container.

Sulfuric acid, also known as battery acid, is another strong acid used in the processing of meth. Sulfuric acid is not flammable but is highly reactive and highly corrosive, especially to human tissue. While sulfuric acid is not flammable, it is capable of reacting with and igniting finely divided combustible materials upon contact. Sulfuric acid also reacts violently with water, producing an exothermic chemical reaction along with high pressure. This is just another example why firefighters should never spray water into a meth lab.

Iodine crystals are the next group we will look at. When heated and released into the air, iodine vapor irritates the respiratory system and eyes. In the solid form, iodine may cause severe irritation and burns upon contact with tissue. It is also very poisonous if ingested. In addition, iodine crystals are incompatible with ammonia and reactive metals such as lithium. This toxin targets the eyes, skin, respiratory system, central nervous system and cardiovascular system in the body.

Red phosphorous is yet another chemical found in these labs. Red phosphorous presents two main types of hazards. First, red phosphorous vapors can irritate the nose, throat, lung and eyes. The secondary danger comes when this material is heated up. When this is heated it turns into white phosphorous. Heating may be accidental, caused by improper storage in a hot area or direct sunlight, or purposely, by using it in a chemical reaction. Either way, white phosphorous ignites spontaneously upon contact with air at or above 30 degrees C (86 degrees F). In addition, white phosphorous is explosive when mixed with oxidizing agents and will produce phosphine gas during combustion. Phosphine gas is known as a pyrophoric gas, meaning that this type of gas will ignite spontaneously upon contact with air.

Lithium metal, often found in watch batteries, is a combustible metal that has several nasty traits. Lithium takes the form of a silver, soft waxy metal which is extremely dangerous upon contact with water. This is due to the fact that the chemical reaction caused by this contact with water produces hydrogen gas. As stated earlier, hydrogen gas is extremely explosive. All that is needed is an ignition source. This ignition source can easily come from the chemical reaction itself. When water and lithium combine, the reaction also generates adequate heat to ignite the hydrogen, causing an explosion. Lithium, under the proper conditions, also has the ability to ignite spontaneously in air.

Other material that is needed to complete the lab is a water source and a heat source. The heat source will normally be electrical, as any open flame in the lab can lead to explosions. In addition, lab beakers and plates are also needed to handle the reactions.

Firefighters are taught to leave an area immediately after identifying the presence of a meth lab because many of the contents of the lab react violently with water, the main extinguishing source for fire departments. Also, interrupting or stopping the reaction may lead to over pressurization of the vessels, explosions or fire. The bottom line for anyone is stay away if you suspect the presence of a meth lab. Call the proper authorities and let the professionals handle the scene.

METH ACT OF 1996

Prior to 1996, the chemicals listed above were fairly easy to obtain. Many were available through the mail, without presenting any real chance of getting caught. But in 1996, the Meth Act of 1996 was put into law. This law restricted the access to many of the raw chemicals needed to produce meth. Many of the sources for the cooks dried up due to this law. If the mail order business did any business, they had to report to the Federal Government the names of the people buying the material. Also, the purchasing of Sudafed® became harder due to this law. Many stores voluntarily restricted the number of boxes sold at any given time. Their registers were designed to lock out if more than a certain number of boxes of Sudafed® were purchased. They then required identification to proceed with the transaction. As a result, the cook had to turn to other means to obtain the needed ingredients (figure 5.5 and 5.6). Another problem then developed. Due to the fact that purchasing laboratory level beakers and dishes was slowed by The Meth Act, secondary sources were used. Instead of heavy duty beakers, made to handle the heat and pressure of the chemical reactions, secondary devices were now being used. Items such as mason jars and plastic containers replaced the lab beakers (figure 5.7 and 5.8). The result is that many of these secondary forms of equipment lead to failure of the vessel and in many cases caused fires and explosions. In an article by *David Peterson dated August 26, 2002,* he states that while most illegal labs are discovered by DEA personnel or local law enforcement efforts, 20 to 30% are found by explosions."

COMMON SOURCE OF CHEMICALS TO MANUFACTURE METH

Toluene	found in paint thinner
Methanol	found in gas tank anti-freeze "Heet"
Ethyl Ether	found in starting fluid
Anhydrous ammonia	found at farmer's co-ops
Hydrochloric acid	found in hardware stores
Ephedrine	found in cold medicine or dietary supplements
Sodium hydroxide	found in "Drano" or Red Devil Lye
Sulfuric acid	found in battery acid or drain cleaners
Iodine crystals	found in iodine crystals or tincture of iodine
Red phosphorous	found in striker plates
Lithium	found in camera batteries

Figure 5.5 Secondary means to obtain needed chemicals

Figure 5.6 cans of lye at Meth lab

Figure 5.7 Examples of secondary forms of lab equipment

Figure 5.8 Examples of secondary forms of lab equipment

STILL MORE HAZARDS AT LABS

If the chemicals and chance of explosions are not enough to keep you away from these labs, the public must realize that up to 90% of these labs may be under the control of Mexican Cartels or other gangs. What this brings into the picture is items such as booby traps and weapons, a method of keeping people away from their operation.

Up to 10% of the labs across the nation contain some form of trap to stop unwelcome guests. There are many forms of traps set for the unsuspecting person. Holes cut in floors, covered by blankets or rugs are common and fairly easy to do. As the unsuspecting person walks on the rug, he then falls into the basement or a hole dug under the rug. Electrical wires, running from a light switch to an open can of gasoline are still another example. By turning on the switch, a spark would be created at the open end of the wires located in the can. This spark would cause ignition of the vapors, resulting in an explosion.

Other examples of traps set by the cooks include nails in boards surrounding the building. These nail protrude through the board and the board is hidden by the grass, point side up. Anyone attempting to approach the building will step on the nails, stopping them in their tracks. Many of these nails could also be coated with chemicals to enhance the effect of the penetration.

Chemical traps are also common in these labs. Hydrochloric acid and cyanide tablets are an example. Hydrochloric acid is placed in a beaker near a main entrance door. Next to the beaker is a plate with cyanide tablets on it. Opening of a door tips over the beaker of hydrochloric acid, mixing the acid with the cyanide tablets. This produces hydrogen cyanide gas, a very strong blood agent and the gas used in gas chambers. Other chemical traps include tear gas canisters tied to monofilament trip line. The intruder trips the line, which activates the canister of tear gas, filling the room.

Two other common traps are animals placed in the house and fish hooks hung on monofilament fishing line. Organized labs have brought in animals such as Pit Bulls or even rattle snakes to be placed on the porch of the building. As the curious person enters the area, these animals provide a very unpleasant surprise. Fish hooks hanging on monofilament line placed at eye level is another trap. The unsuspecting person walks into the room and catches these hooks in the eye or face, causing severe pain and injury.

Lastly, weapons have become very popular at meth labs. The labs, run by organized Cartels or just paranoid cooks, may have large numbers of weapons. These weapons are easily obtained and the ammunition is readily available through the mail. The end result is a large amount of fire power (figure 5.9). Along with automatic weapons, pipe bombs are easily made and can be easily deployed in case of a raid. The major ingredients for these bombs can be purchased by going to three types of stores. First a hardware store to obtain the pipe and pipe caps a sporting goods store to obtain the powder and lastly a hobby shop to purchase the fuse. Once all the items are bought, the recipe is easily obtained on the internet. One major drawback to pipe bombs is that the manufacturing process used to make these bombs is very dangerous and one incorrect move can result in the maker loosing many parts of his body (Figure 5.10).

Figure 5.9 Automatic weapons found at labs

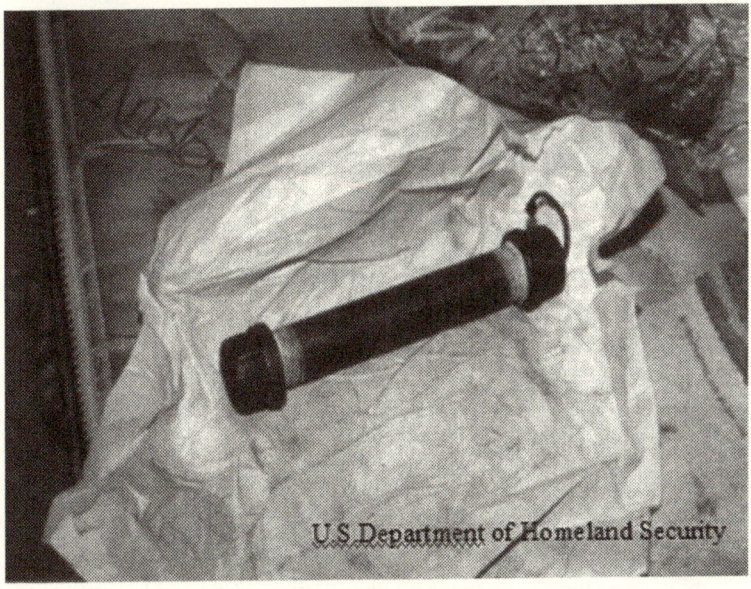

Figure 5.10 pipe bomb found at Meth lab

CHAPTER 6

▼

HOW TO HANDLE
METH LABS

In this chapter, I will be looking at the labs in several ways. First, I will concentrate on what the Government is doing to handle this epidemic. Secondly, I will look at options that are available to Emergency Responders. Third, I will talk about the general public, and what should be done if anyone thinks that a meth lab is present in the area. Lastly, I will try to give some advice on what to do if someone thinks that a loved one is actually using this drug. This portion may be the most important part of this book.

ACTIONS AT THE TOP

Many laws were enacted, both on the Federal and State levels to combat the meth crisis. I will cover some of the major actions that have been taken to help cure this menace.

First of all, *The Meth Act of 1996*. This act, as previously stated, was an attempt to stop the producers of the drug from obtaining needed material for the manufacture of the meth. The concept of the law is good, and many stores voluntarily limited the sales of products like Sudafed®. But as with any market, it did not take long to find ways around this law. The cooks, with the help of internet chemists, found ways to extract needed chemicals from other sources. In addition, even though the sale of Sudafed® was controlled in the United States, secondary markets developed. A recent sting operation showed that our neighbors to the north, Canada, may be a supplier of these needed tablets to the users. An article on *foxnews.com dated September 1, 2002*, outlines a sting operation called Operation Mountain Express III, (Figure 6.1).

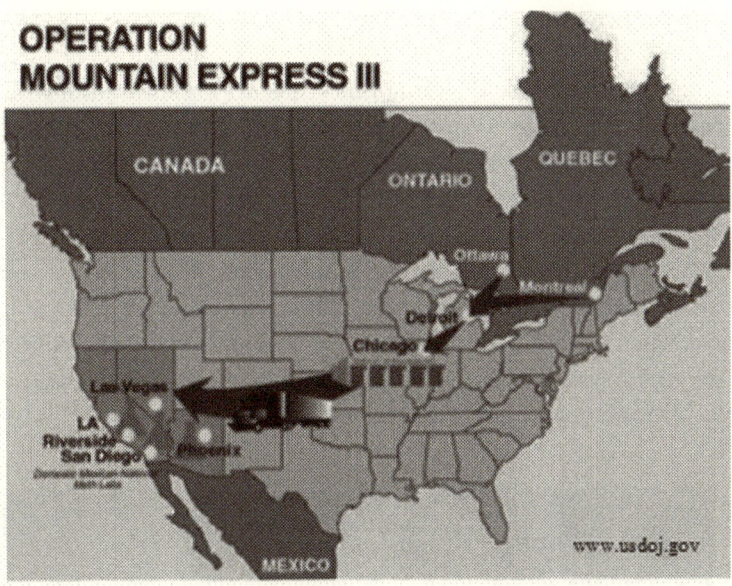

Figure 6.1 Operation Mountain Express III

This drug raid was conducted on January 10, 2002. Arrests were made in Detroit, Cleveland, Chicago and Phoenix. The sting operation resulted in charges being brought against 136 people, a seizure of 36 tons of pseudoephedrine, 179 pounds of meth, $4.5 million dollars in cash, eight real estate properties and 160 automobiles.

Most of the men arrested were smuggling large quantities of pseudoephedrine from Canada, where this medication is not regulated. The U.S. drug ring was then reselling this product to Mexican base drug operations located in the Midwest. If the operation was not disturbing enough, the money from the sale of the pseudoephedrine was being diverted to Middle East terrorist groups.

A recent act by President George Bush, called the *Combat Meth Act of 2005*, would make the purchase limit of 7.5 grams of pseudoephedrine a national standard to follow. This act would also require retailers to keep these products behind pharmacy counters. In addition, this bill requires signatures and personal identification for the purchase of this medication. The hope is to keep this base ingredient out of the hand of the cooks, and by standardizing the amount allowed to be purchased, keeping the cooks from going over state lines to obtain the product from a more lenient state.

In an attempt to provide the Drug Enforcement Administration with the necessary resources, the *Methamphetamine Anti-Proliferation Act* became law in 2000. This act is a comprehensive measure that provided additional money to support the training of additional DEA and special agents to fight the spread of meth. The *Methamphetamine Anti-Proliferation Act* has allowed the DEA to increase the number of special agents used in tracking down and processing meth labs. This increase has allowed more special agents to be available to help local authorities when a lab is found. The DEA requests that they be notified of any meth labs that are found, and with the drastic increase of labs, the increase in manpower was needed (Figure 6.2, and 6.3).

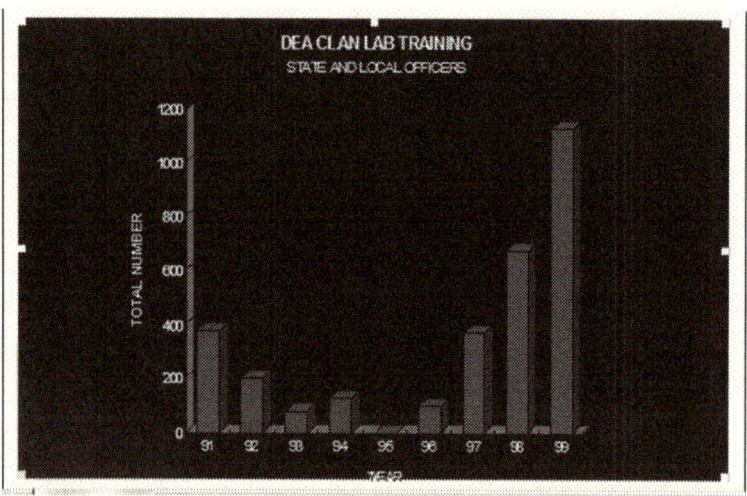

Figure 6.2 Speical DEA agents

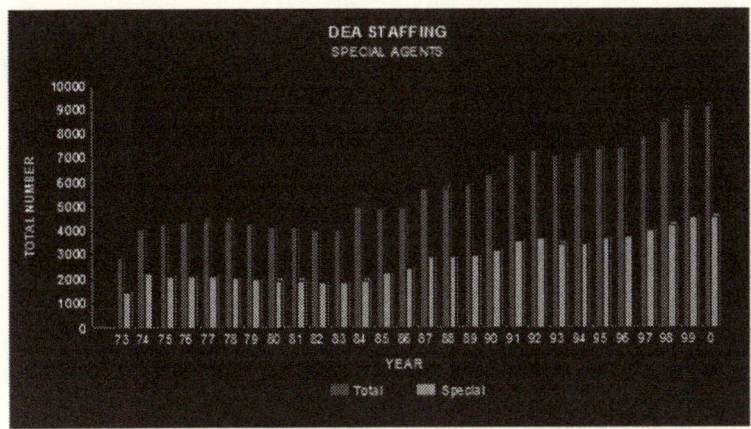

Figure 6.3 State Officers trained by DEA

Actions at the State level

Several states, including Wisconsin, are taking a proactive approach to the growing problem. The theft of anhydrous ammonia, a key ingredient in the manufacture of meth, is now a felony in Wisconsin. On April 4, 2001, Governor Scott McCallum signed legislation that makes the theft of anhydrous ammonia a felony. State Law now would penalize thieves with a **3 1/2-year prison sentence**, **a fine of up to** **$10,000 or both**. The penalty would also extend to **transferring the product** to containers that do not meet state specifications, such as propane tanks.

Additional legislation by Governor Jim Doyle, dated June 22, 2005, now makes it a felony to purchase more than 7.5 grams of medication containing ephedrine or pseudoephedrine. The Meth Act of 1996 initially limited sales of this medication to 24 grams. This new State law restricts the sales even further. Wisconsin now joins seven other states that have adopted this policy of restricting the sale of this medication:

Arizona	Missouri
Arkansas	Texas
Iowa	West Virginia
Kansas	Wisconsin

It is important to realize that these actions by the eight states mentioned above came before the Federal Government started action on the *Combat Meth Act*, showing how proactive these states are.

Voluntary Action by Retailers

In addition to these tougher laws, a number of major retailers have also taken voluntary action to limit access to cold medicine containing pseudoephedrine:

Target	CVS
Wal-mart	K-Mart
Albertson's	Shopko
Rite-Aid	Longs Drugs
Walgreen's	Safeway

Voluntary Action by Manufacturers

Several manufacturers have made an attempt to support the government's efforts to stop the production of meth. One product that was used extensively in the past for the manufacture of meth was Dexatrim®. Dexatrim® is an over the counter weight loss product that used the same ingredients that makes Sudafed® so popular to the cooks. Several years ago, Dexatrim® changed their recipe and now uses caffeine as the main ingredient.

The manufactures of Sudafed® are in the process of also changing their recipe for their product. The removal of this main ingredient from the market would greatly reduce the availability of ephedrine or pseudoephedrine to the cooks, hopefully putting a dent in the meth market.

EMERGENCY RESPONDERS

Being an emergency responder myself, I have a great appreciation for the dangers these labs present. Therefore, it is imperative that any responder, be it Police, Fire, or EMS have a plan on how to handle any labs they come across. Failure to approach these scenes in the proper manner will lead to injury, exposure or even death to the responder. In an article on *firehouse.com by David Peterson*, he breaks down the injuries to first responders from these Meth labs (Figure 6.4).

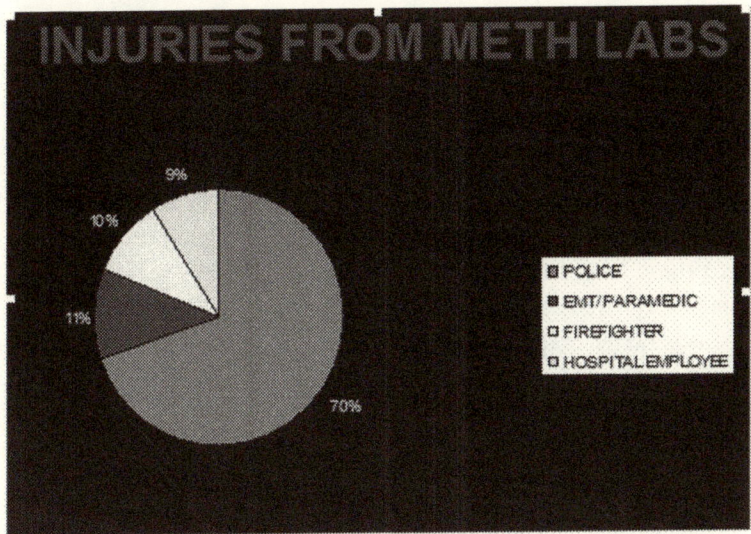

Figure 6.4 Injuries to first responders

In the same article, Peterson outlined the types of injuries that first responders encountered. The major type of injury received by exposure to meth labs has been respiratory irritation, accounting for 54.1% of the injuries to the first responder. In 85.1% of the cases involving first responders, it was reported that proper personal protective was not being worn at the time. This is a major problem. If the police follow a suspect into a building, by the time they realize the environment they are in it may be too late. This is why proper training in lab detection and recognition of signs is a must to avoid exposure.

Another necessity for any responding agency is establishing proper departmental procedures to follow when these labs are detected. In the fire service, we use Standard Operating Procedures (SOP's), or Standard Operating Guidelines (SOG's). Whatever the procedures are called, they provide a standardized way to approach these labs. They may also protect the responder from possible litigation in the future. Many of these guidelines list, in writing, that defensive actions are an acceptable alternative to actively attacking a fire in a lab. The reasons for a defensive action are obvious, but in a court case, having a written procedure may prove beneficial to the fire crews who were at the scene

There are many sources for obtaining information on SOP's for your department. One of the best I have found is the Phoenix Fire Department. They provide full access to their entire SOP collection and are there for other departments to use. The Phoenix Fire Department web site is www.phoenix.gov\fire.

It is imperative that when a meth lab is found, the DEA be notified. There are several reasons for this requirement. The DEA requires their presence at the scene of these labs. Any meth lab must be considered both a hazardous material scene as well as a crime scene. These federal agents are specially trained to handle and investigate these labs. In addition, the DEA will normally handle the cleanup operations. With the cost of cleanup approaching $50,000 per lab, the federal government is better prepared to handle this cost. They may use local hazardous material teams to assist, but the DEA will still be handling most of the scene operations.

The most important thing to remember as a first responder is not to touch anything or apply water to the scene, as many of the chemicals are water reactive. Power, water or any other service must not be cut. Entry into the lab must be restricted and a proper perimeter must be established to handle any onlookers. Any of the people in harms way should be evacuated to a safe distance, if evacuation can be conducted safely. The last item is the user themselves. Even though the user may seem thin and weak, the user is normally very strong. This is because the meth in their system gives them a large amount of energy. If the user gets hold of the responder, the results could be disastrous. The responder should keep a distance of at least 7 to 10 feet. The users "personal space" is larger than a non-user's. Maintaining a larger than normal safety zone will tend to keep the user calm and will keep you out of harms way.

Never should a responder shine a light at the user. The user has probably been on meth for quite a while and has not seen the light of day for some time. This coupled with the fact that pupil dilation is a common side effect of the drug, a light shining at him could be like him seeing a train coming down a tunnel. This could lead to drastic action on the part of the user.

When talking to the meth user, the responder must slow down his speech pattern and lower the pitch of his voice. The user's mind is racing due to the meth. A fast speech pattern or a loud approach will seem threatening to the user. In addition, the use of meth has probably made the user very paranoid. The responder, in addition to slowing down his speech must also slow down his movements and keep his hands visible at all times. At no time should the responder make a move towards the meth user. Any fast movements on the responder's part would seem extremely threatening to the user and could cause the user to go off the deep end.

Lastly, it is important to keep the user talking. At this point the mind of the addicted person is one dimensional. If he is talking to you and making eye contact, chances are that he is not thinking of something else. By keeping the user talking, you are at least controlling his thoughts. You may not be able to overcome the effects of the meth, namely paranoia, but at least he is not thinking of any secondary action. If, on the other hand, the user starts looking around, he is probably planning some kind of action, either getting a weapon or he may be getting ready to make a move. Try to keep the user talking until adequate personal arrive on the scene to properly handle the situation.

THE GENERAL PUBLIC

Throughout this book I have been talking about the hazards of the drug, the hazards of the labs and the dangers of the users themselves. The best advice I can give to anyone who thinks there is a lab in his or her area is to **STAY AWAY!!!!!!!!!** Anyone who wanders too near this lab faces the chance of getting injured, either by the user, traps, or the chemicals themselves. The best thing to do is to call the local police department and wait for them to respond. Allow the professionals to do the work. This is what we are trained for. Basically, any actions on your part will probably do more harm than good. Again, as I say in my classes, **WHEN IN DOUBT, STAY OUT!**

WHAT IF A LOVED ONE MAY BE USING METH?

This is a tough subject to deal with. The truth of the matter is the best defense is a good offense. In this case, the best way to get your loved one off meth is to make sure they never try meth. I know that this is easy to say and hard to do, but the best thing to do is keep communicating with your loved one, and make sure they know the dangers of meth. As was mentioned earlier, "The younger the age of drug initiation, the greater the likelihood the drug use will become an addiction and the more difficult it becomes to stop the use later on". Many young people feel that they are invincible. They feel that they can handle the drug. They have to be convinced that this is one drug that will control them, very early in the process. Many agencies, such as The National Clearinghouse for Alcohol and Drug Information and The National Institute on Drug Abuse are just two of many sites that will provide literature at no cost to anyone who may seek help. In addition to these agencies, a web site, www.kci.org/meth is an excellent resource for help. This site, known as KCI The Anti-Meth Site, formally known as The Koch Crime Institute, provided me with a great deal of information on meth. This site will tie you into letters and stories, meth chat rooms and meth message boards. In addition, this site will also provide access to other sites that will help a person obtain more information about meth. Written information on meth along with videos and even PowerPoint® presentations are available, many at no cost. The more information a person has on this drug, the more help they can be to anyone who is trapped in the clutches of meth.

If you suspect that someone you know is on meth remember that they need help right away. Meth presents a very slippery slope to operate from. By the time many seek help, damage has already occurred to the brain. The damage to the brain caused by meth use is similar to damage caused by Alzheimer's disease, stroke, and epilepsy. They will need immediate medical attention to get the proper medication to offset the effects of meth. In addition, they will also need a professional psychiatrist or psychologist to help get their life back in order. If their friends are using meth, these are not the people for your loved one to talk to. Your family doctor should be able to direct you to the proper person to help your loved one back on the road to recovery. Your loved one will normally have to change their circle of friends. Users do not normally have friends, they have fellow users. A close circle of supportive friends will help in the recovery.

This is like any illness, with the proper support and help, recovery will come. One major hurdle you will face is that when the user is trying to kick the habit, they will have the urge to relapse back to their former lifestyle. This is a common occurrence among meth users. During an interview on a recent Montel show, a former user was being interviewed. She admitted to selling herself for drug money and sleeping in dumpsters and cardboard boxes. Even though she had been off the drug for several weeks, all she wanted to do was to get high and go back to her former drug life. This is when the addicts really need the professional support, to help them over this painful period of recovery.

Lastly, they are going to need your love and support. The person you may see in front of you is not the real person you love. This is a person who is sick, who has been taken over by a drug that will kill without any remorse. This loved one is facing a very long and lonely road to recovery. The truth is that once addicted; only 10% of meth users actually fully recover from the drug. Your support throughout the recovery process is essential for a successful outcome. Realize that the recovery may take months, even years, and even if both of you stick it out and the addict stays on the path to recovery, success may be a long way down the road. But this course of action is still better than the alternative life of drug addiction. It is better than giving up everything you own just to get another hit of meth. It is better than watching your body wasting away and your teeth falling out of your mouth. It is better than walking around like a zombie, suffering from paranoia and other mental disorders. And it is definitely better than dying.

Good luck and May God Bless you in your efforts.

BIBLIOGRAPHY

Anonymous. Personal Interview. 11 November, 2002

"Crystal Meth: Killing Our Youth." The Montel Show. NBC.WGBA, Green Bay. 12 May 2005.

Eskridge, Chris, and, Brandon Paeper. "The Mexican Cartels: A Challenge for the 21st Century."Criminal Organizations, Vol 12.5 (1998): 5–15. 16 Feb. 2002 <http://www.unl.edu>.

FoxNews.com. U.S. Drug Money Funded Terror Group, DEA Says. 1 Sept. 2002. 1 Sept. 2002 <http.foxnews.com/printer_friendly_story/ 0,3566,61848,00.html>.

Hanson, Glen. The Neurobiology of Addiction, What Does it mean for Children & Adolescents. Dec. 2005 <http://www.nida.hih.gov>.

Harlic, Jeanene."Byproducts of "cooking" Hurt Children." Meth the devil's drug. 14 Sept. 2002 <http://www.redding.com/specials/meth>.

Institute for Intergovernmental Research. The Methamphetamine Problem: A Question and Answer Guide. 4 Dec. 2005 <www.iir.com>.

Koch Crime Institute. Methamphetamine Frequently Asked Questions. 28 Jan. 2002 <http://www.kci.org/meth_info>.

Korlantzick, Josh. "Yaba: The New Drug War." Today's Officer. 18 Sept. 2004. Sept 2004 <http://www.moaa.org/TodaysOfficer/Military/yaba_1>.

—. "Yaba: The New Drug War." Today's Officer. 18 Sept. 2004. Sept 2004 <http://www.moaa.org/TodaysOfficer/Military/yaba_2>.

—. "Yaba: The New Drug War." Today's Officer. 18 Sept. 2004. Sept 2004 <http://www.moaa.org/TodaysOfficer/Military/yaba_3>.

Lamb, David. "Rival to heroin is Thailand's new Nemesis." Cannabis News. 26 Nov. 1999. 18 Sept. 2004 <http://www.cannabisnews.com>.

Miller, Jenny. "County board hears meth presentation." Barron News Shield. 5 Jul. 2005. 7 Dec. 2005 <http://www.zwire.com>.

"The Most Dangerous Man in America." 48 Hours: Target: Terror. CBS. WFRV, Green Bay. 30 Jan. 2002.

Multnomah County Sheriff's Office. "Faces of Meth Mug Shots from the Faces of Meth 2005 V 1 CD." Dec. 2005 <www.facesofmeth.us>.

National Institute on Drug Abuse. "How is Methamphetamine different from other stimulants, such as cocaine?" Research Report Series—Methamphetamine Abuse and Addiction. 28 Nov. 2005 <http://www.nida.nih.gov>.

National Propane Gas Association. Anhydrous Ammonia Safety Alert, Anhydrous ammonia and propane cylinders. 8 Dec 2005 <http://www.npga.org>.

Office of Attorney General Terry Goddard. Methamphetamine Fact Sheet. Dec. 2005 <www.azag.gov>.

Office of National Drug Control Policy. Methamphetamine Fact Sheet. 30 Nov 2005. Nov 2003 <http://www.whitehousedrugpolicy.gov>.

Peterson, David. "Hazardous Materials—Clandestine Drug Labs." Firenuggets.com 26 Aug. 2002. 7 Oct. 2002 <http://www.firehouse.com/training/hazmat>.

Prairie View Prevention Services, Inc. Meth Awareness and Prevention Project. Dec. 2005<http://www.mappsd.org>.

Smith, James. "Mexican drug cartels thrive under new breed of traffickers." Kansas City Star. 5 Dec. 1999. 17 Feb. 2002 <http://www.kcstar.com>.

Tweaked. Video produced by The Foundation.

United States. Dept. of Health and Human Services. Natl. Inst. of Health. "Methamphetamine: Abuse and Addiction." NIH Publication Number 98-4210. Apr. 1998. Apr. 2005 <http://www.nida.nih.gov>.

—Dept. of Justice. Natl. Drug Intelligence Center. Yaba Fast Facts. June 2003. 18 Sept. 2004 <http://www.usdoj.gov/ndic/pubs5/5048>.

—Drug Enforcement Administration. Briefs & Background, Drugs and Drug Abuse, "State Factsheet, Wisconsin" 19 Dec. 2005. 2005 <http://www.dea.gov/pubs/states/wisconsinp.html>.

—Drug Enforcement Administration. Drug Trafficking in the United States. 12 Dec. 2005 <http://www.dea.gov/concern/drug_trafficking.html>.

—Drug Enforcement Administration. United States. Dept. of Justice. More Than 100 Arrested in Nationwide Methamphetamine Investigation. 10 Jan 2002. 12 Dec 2005 <http://www.usdoj.gov>.

Where Meth Goes, Violence & Destruction Follows. Video provided by the California Dept. of Justice.

Wikipedia. The Free Encyclopedia. Meth Mouth. 31 Oct. 2005. 7 Dec. 2005 <http://en.wikipedia.org>.

978-0-595-38440-2
0-595-38440-4